Protecting WILD ANIMALS

By Jim Aaron
Illustrated by Anil Ampur

W9-CEP-374

Scott Foresman
is an imprint of

PEARSON

Glenview, Illinois • Boston, Massachusetts • Chandler, Arizona •
Upper Saddle River, New Jersey

Photographs

Every effort has been made to secure permission and provide appropriate credit for photographic material. The publisher deeply regrets any omission and pledges to correct errors called to its attention in subsequent editions.

Unless otherwise acknowledged, all photographs are the property of Pearson Education, Inc.

20 Juniors Bildarchiv/Alamy Images.

ISBN 13: 978-0-328-51630-8
ISBN 10:   0-328-51630-9

4 5 6 7 8 9 10 V0FL 14 13 12 11

Ezra's summer plans were ruined. He wanted to go to baseball camp so that he could perfect his pitch. He wanted to practice his dives at the town pool.

Instead, he was stuck in this van with his family. Ezra, his sister, and his parents were driving to a wildlife center where they would live for the summer, far away from home. Ezra still couldn't get used to the idea. He didn't *want* to get used to it.

"It will be great, Ezzie," said Dad. "You've always said that you wanted to go to work with Mom and me. Now here's your chance."

His parents were scientists who studied wild animals. Ezra thought about the center and tried to smile.

Rosa, Ezra's big sister, on the other hand, was thrilled about this adventure. In fact, she was so excited that she could barely stop asking questions. She wanted to know how long they would stay and where they would live. She wanted to know what kinds of animals were there and whether she could touch them.

"How do animals wind up at the center?" she asked.

"They may be sick," said Mom, "or injured. The people there take care of them, nurse them back to health, and help them return to the wild."

"Sometimes baby animals are found. They may have lost or gotten separated from their mothers," said Dad. "They're too young to be on their own. They need to be fed and taught how to live in the wild."

"I hope I can take care of some of the babies," Rosa sighed dreamily.

Ezra had to admit, it did sound interesting. He put his earphones back on and listened to some music. After a while, he dozed off. It was a long trip to the center.

He woke to a loud chorus of honks. There must have been twenty or more geese flocked in front of the van.

Rosa laughed. "Road hogs!" she said.

Ezra rubbed his eyes.

"I've heard about these geese," said Dad. "Nothing scares them. They like to come out and welcome visitors to the center."

Ezra noticed a handmade sign beside the road that read "Western Wildlife Preserve." It was pointing straight ahead where, under the grove of pine trees, huddled a bunch of rustic cabins. None of them had satellite dishes.

"No TV?" he groaned.

Dad turned, smiled, and ruffled Ezra's hair. "I think you'll find much better things to do."

A woman met them at the office. "Hi!" she greeted them cheerfully.

Mom introduced them. "Hi, Nikki. I want to introduce you to Rosa and Ezra."

"I'm glad to meet you and so happy that you could join your parents here," Nikki said.

Ezra stared, fascinated, at the creature perched on Nikki's shoulder. It was a chipmunk!

"This is Cassie," Nikki said, noticing where Ezra was staring. She gently patted its head and continued, "Her den is under the side of this building, but more often than not she's here with me." Nikki pointed to a bowl on her desk. "You can give her an acorn, if you'd like."

"Go on, Ezzie," Rosa nudged.

Ezra took an acorn and slowly put it near the chipmunk's nose. Cassie stood up on her hind legs and snatched the acorn with her tiny front paws. She ate it so quickly that it made him laugh.

"She *is* funny, isn't she?" said Nikki.

Ezra nodded and then looked down at his suitcases. He wasn't sure he wanted to give the impression that he was enjoying himself.

Nikki volunteered to walk Erza and his family to their cabin. It was small—so much smaller than their house. Inside there was a single living area with roughly made wooden furniture, three tiny bedrooms, and one bathroom. A single bookcase in the living room was brimming with books about all sorts of animals.

"We need to meet Dr. Margaret, the veterinarian in charge," said Mom. "You kids can come with us if you'd like."

"I can also take them on a tour of the center," Nikki offered. "I'll introduce them to some of the animals. How does that sound?" she asked the kids.

"Great!" Rosa said, practically shouting.

Ezra nodded. He didn't want to seem impolite.

"Thanks, Nikki," said Dad. "We'll meet you back here for dinner, kids."

How can we eat dinner without a kitchen? Ezra wondered.

"Have you guys ever seen a baby badger before?" Nikki asked them. "Eight of them were brought to us last week. They were rescued from their den in a river bank. We think they may have been abandoned by their mother."

"Oh, that's awful!" Rosa said.

"I know. They're fine now, however, and as cute as can be."

They went down a path that led to another cabin. A man met them at the door.

"Come on in," he said. "We're feeding the little guys right now."

Just then, a small, furry creature waddled past Ezra's feet. Ezra jumped back.

"Oh, don't worry. She's just looking for her bottle."

"Jack," Nikki said to the man, "can our friends help with the feeding?"

"Sure!" Jack said.

He brought Ezra and Rosa small bottles of milk and showed them where to sit. Then he gently scooped the little badger up and gave it to Rosa. After a few tries, she got the bottle positioned correctly, and the young animal began to drink greedily.

"Wow, she's really hungry!" Rosa said.

"The badgers have grown so much since they came here," Nikki observed.

"This one is bigger than our cat," said Rosa.

"In about another month, we'll release them back into the wild," Jack said.

Ezra leaned closer. He patted the badger's bristled head.

"Can I try feeding her?" he asked.

"Wait a second," said Jack. "There's another one I had in mind for you, but first we must catch him!"

Ezra put down the bottle and rose from his chair. He followed Jack into the other room. There were two badger babies playing on a soft blanket.

"Those guys ate already," Jack said. "The one we're looking for likes to play hide-and-seek before he eats."

Suddenly, Ezra saw a fuzzy tail disappear around a corner. "There he goes!" Ezra said. He leapt forward and chased the badger into the kitchen.

The only animal in the kitchen was a cat sleeping on a patched blanket. A moment later, Ezra heard a scurrying sound on the basement steps. He went to the doorway and looked down the stairs. Shiny black eyes peered up at him.

"It's okay, little guy. I just want to give you your dinner." Ezra kept his voice low. He lifted his foot and gently, as if in slow motion, placed it on the first step.

The badger sniffed the air.

Maybe he's curious about me, Ezra thought as he squatted down.

The next thing Ezra knew, he'd lifted the wriggly critter into his hands and carried him back into the room. Nikki and Jack applauded, and then Jack handed Ezra the bottle of milk.

"This is really fun," Ezra commented.

"See?" Rosa said. "I *knew* you'd like coming here."

Ezra wasn't so sure about that yet. Just because he'd enjoyed feeding a badger didn't mean he'd want to spend the whole summer doing this. He did, however, have to admit that there was something about these silvery-haired creatures that fascinated him.

After the badgers drank their fill, Jack asked, "Would you two like to see where we found them?"

Ezra and Rosa nodded.

Jack led the way outside. They followed a wooded path toward the sound of a splashing river.

"That was their den," Jack said when they reached the river's bank. "The babies were snug inside, but they were missing their mother."

"Do you know what happened to her?" Ezra asked.

Jack shook his head. "She wasn't there. She was probably sick or injured. It's hard to know for sure."

After that, Nikki showed the kids around the other parts of the wildlife center. She introduced them to the bald eagle. It had a broken wing and stayed in a huge wire cage where it could move freely. She took them to see other wild birds, including some that had just been rescued from an oil spill. Then she guided them to the reptiles and amphibians.

Ezra watched a turtle hobbling toward its food on its short, jointed legs. "What happened to it?" he asked.

"It stumbled into an animal trap," Nikki said.

"Poor thing," Rosa replied, shaking her head.

"Yes," Nikki agreed. "That one will spend its whole life here."

Ezra wasn't sure that was so bad. The turtle had a nice pond, and it would be safe here.

By the time Ezra and Rosa got back to the cabin, the sun was setting. Their parents were busy unpacking.

"How was your afternoon?" asked Dad.

"Excellent!" Rosa said enthusiastically.

"Pretty good," Ezra admitted.

While he finished unpacking his suitcase, he realized that he really meant it. The day had been more than pretty good. It had been, as Rosa said, excellent.

The question was *what would happen tomorrow?*

In the meantime, the family walked over to another building that served as the dining hall for the center. Ezra was surprised by how many people he saw there. He was also surprised by how good the food was. He was so hungry that he had three helpings of chicken, carrots, and rice.

The days seemed to melt into one. Ezra and Rosa spent their mornings working with the animals. In the afternoons, they went hiking with their parents or swimming at a nearby lake. At night, Ezra usually read a book for a few minutes before falling fast asleep. He barely even thought about TV.

Most mornings, Ezra stayed with the badgers.

"Let's work on their hunting skills today," Jack told him one sunny day.

They brought two badgers outside into the fenced yard. One was the little badger Ezra had fed on his first day at the center. Ezra had named him "Rascal."

Jack had caught a snake in the woods. Now he set it free, and it wriggled through the grass. At first, the badgers didn't seem to know what to do. But then, as their natural instincts took over, they chased and eventually caught the snake.

The weeks flew by. The badgers grew more and more comfortable outdoors. They also became better hunters. One day, Dr. Margaret finally felt that the badgers were ready to return to the wild.

She and Jack coaxed the badgers into a large wooden box and loaded it onto the back of a four-wheeler. Then they led the procession of people down to the bank of the river. They unloaded the crate there in the same location where the orphaned badgers had first been found.

Dr. Margaret opened the sliding door. Gradually, the badgers waddled out into the sunlight, squeaking loudly, unsure of what to do. At first, Rascal ran around in circles! And then, as if on cue, the badgers scurried off in every direction. Rascal ran into the rushes and disappeared.

A big cheer went up.

Ezra looked at his new friends cheering. He thought back to how sad he had been about coming here. Now he felt sad to see the badgers go, but he was also happy. He'd helped them return to where they belonged. And he knew he'd found a place where *he* belonged too.

Rescuing Wild Animals

There are many wild animal rescue centers throughout the United States. The Wildlife Rehabilitation Center in Roseville, Minnesota, is one of these places. More than 8,500 animals—including songbirds, waterfowl, mammals, and reptiles—are treated there. Almost half of these are baby animals that need to be fed around the clock.

Animals are brought to the center mainly because of some human-made problem. For instance, in spring of 2008, several young red fox kits were brought to the center. Their coats were covered with a toxic chemical that came from a factory. The staff cleaned them, fed them, and taught them how to hunt. Two months later, the kits were returned to their wilderness home.

Across the country, animals are rescued through the efforts of wildlife centers like this one.

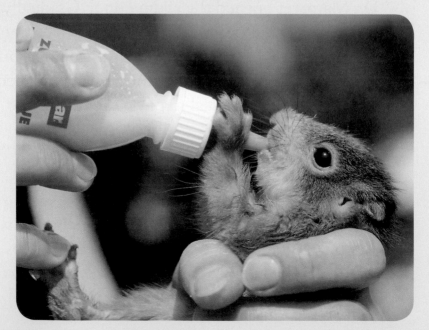